W9-BRC-338

AFRICA
ACTIVITY BOOK
ART, CRAFTS, HISTORICAL AIDS

Written by	Robyn Hamilton
Edited by	Kathy Rogers
Design by	Linda Milliken
Illustrated by	Barb Lorseyedi

METRIC CONVERSION CHART
Refer to this chart when metric conversions are not found within the activity.

4 tsp	= 1 ml	4 cup	= 60 ml	350° F =	180° C	1 inch	=	2.54 cm
2 tsp	= 2 ml	3 cup	= 80 ml	375° F =	190° C	1 foot	=	30 cm
1 tsp	= 5 ml	2 cup	= 125 ml	400° F =	200° C	1 yard	=	91 cm
1 Tbsp	= 15 ml	1 cup	= 250 ml	425° F =	216° C	1 mile	=	1.6 km
			1 oz.	=	28 g			
			1 lb.	=	.45 kg			

EP071 • ©1996 Edupress, Inc. • P.O. Box 883 • Dana Point, CA 92629
www.edupressinc.com

ISBN 1-56472-071-3
Printed in USA

TABLE OF CONTENTS

GLOSSARY

adinkra cloth—woven cloth that is stamped with designs in ink. Each design has a special meaning.

adire—a method of fabric design in which the cloth is tie-dyed.

batik—a form of fabric design that uses melted wax to help form the dyed designs.

caravan—a group of people traveling together for safety, especially across a desert.

dashiki—a loosely-fitting shirt with an open neck and flowing sleeves. Dashikis are worn by African men for religious ceremonies and festivals.

Eunoto—a ceremony that is held in Masai tribes every seven years. At the *Eunoto* ceremony, warriors are chosen to be tribal elders.

Galimoto—a push toy that African children make from materials they find at hand. It is usually made from scraps of wood and pieces of metal, and resembles a car, motorcycle, or truck.

gele—wrapped headdress worn by African women.

Gold Coast—the southwest part of the country of Ghana. It was named for its rich deposits of gold, first found in the fifteenth century.

grassland—a savanna, a flat, open region or plain without trees.

grisgris—silver good luck charms, or amulets, made and worn by the Taureg people.

ishaka—a musical instrument made of long tubes of straw or sugar cane filled with seeds, beans, pebbles, or sand. It is played by being shaken.

ivory—the hard, creamy-white substance that forms the tusks, horns, and teeth of animals like the hippopotamus and the elephant.

kente cloth—brilliantly colored cloth that is made by weaving complex pattern in strips, and then sewing the strips together.

Mankala—a game in which game pieces are moved from cup to cup. It is also known as *Oware*, *Ayi*, or *Ware*.

Nile River—the longest river in the world. It flows in eastern Africa, through Egypt into the Mediterranean.

Nok—a West African civilization that flourished from 500 B.C. to 200 A.D. The Nok created the oldest known African sculptures.

Nomad—member of a tribe or people that has no fixed home but keeps moving about looking for food or pasture for its animals.

raffia—a straw-like fiber that is used for weaving. It is made from the leaves of special palm trees.

rain forest—a dense, evergreen forest in a rainy tropical area.

Sahara Desert—the world's largest desert, covering most of Northern Africa.

savanna—a flat, open region or plain without trees.

shekere—a musical instrument made from a dried gourd that is wrapped in loose mesh. Beads are attached to the mesh. The *shekere* is shaken.

soapstone—a soft stone that is used for carving household utensils and African figures.

AFRICA

LAND

The continent of Africa is the second largest continent after Asia. It covers about 11,714,000 square miles (30,339,000 km). Climate and geography have significantly shaped African history and culture. Even today these factors are a hindrance and barrier to the free movement of people.

The continent itself is an immense plateau broken by narrow mountain ranges and coastal plains. The longest river in the world, the Nile, flows through northeast Africa. In the northern section is also found the world's largest desert, the Sahara. In the southwestern Congo region are some of the densest rain forests in the world. Much of the continent is grassland inhabited by a diverse animal population.

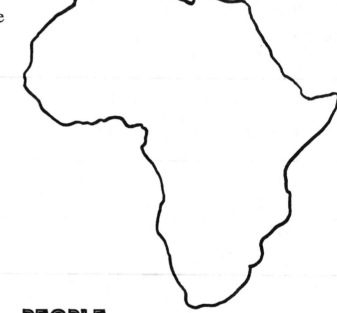

PEOPLE

The majority of the African people live in rural areas much as their ancestors did hundreds of years ago. They have learned to live on the land and use its resources in many ways. Some, like the Masai of the savanna, are cattle herders. The Tuang tribes of the the Sahara are nomads, still following caravans across the desert as their ancestors have done for centuries. Pygmies of the rain forests live by hunting and by gathering forest plants and fruit.

When European traders first began buying from Africans, they wanted gold and ivory. They soon found it more profitable to buy and sell African people. Probably more than 12 million men, women and children were taken from their homes and sold into captivity.

AFRICA

VILLAGES AND CITIES

Homes built from earth, wood, grass, animal hides and skins are still built all over Africa. Homes may be in a village or town, or isolated in farmlands. In the desert, the home of a nomad is a movable tent made of leather stretched across a framework of poles. Pygmies of the rain forest build dome-shaped frameworks of saplings covered with leaves.

There are also enormous cities teeming with modern buildings reflecting the life styles of the Europeans who have settled there.

ART AND CULTURE

The earliest African art known are the drawings and paintings on smooth rock surviving in caves and rock shelters. Africans often decorate the everyday objects they use in their homes, such as plates and bowls. Items made for use in worship ceremonies are valued for their appearance. Objects used in the homes of kings and chiefs—stools, chairs, headrests, bowls, cups, trays—are finely carved and decorated. In some parts of Africa utensils and figures are carved from a very soft stone called *soapstone*. Baskets are woven everywhere in Africa, often beautifully decorated. Sometimes the walls of mud houses are used like an artist's canvas and covered with drawings and paintings. Music is a valued part of daily life. With music, goes dancing. Members of secret societies use masks and clothing of grass or raffia in ceremonial dances. Many African songs are work songs, sung while the soil is hoed or grain is ground into flour. Children have all kinds of singing games with clapping and jumping.

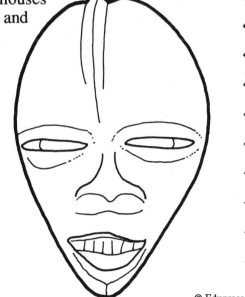

GEOGRAPHY

Historical Aid

At the extreme northwest and southeast of Africa are young mountain ranges. But most of the continent consists of vast flat lands or plateaus having many rivers and streams. Deserts cover nearly forty percent of the continent. The Sahara, in northern Africa, is the largest desert in the world. Savannas, or grasslands, cover another forty percent of the continent. The savannas reach from south of the Sahara to the Congo Basin.

The remainder of the continent consists of rain forests, located in the Congo Basin and in parts of Western Africa and Madagascar. Narrow mountain ranges and long winding rivers also add to the rugged terrain of the African continent.

PROJECT

Create a cooperative mural that illustrates the topographic regions of the African continent.

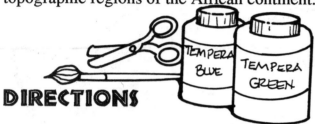

DIRECTIONS

1. Tape butcher paper to the wall and use the overhead projector to magnify the map of Africa to trace on the butcher paper.

2. Lay the large map on a table or the ground and let the students paint the topography of Africa on the map. Use yellow for the deserts, light green for the savannas and dark green for the rain forests.

3. Cut out and display on the bulletin board for use in the animal activity that follows.

MATERIALS

• White butcher paper.

• Topographical map of Africa, following page

• Scissors

• Tempera paint in green, yellow and dark green

• Paint brushes

• Overhead projector

GEOGRAPHY

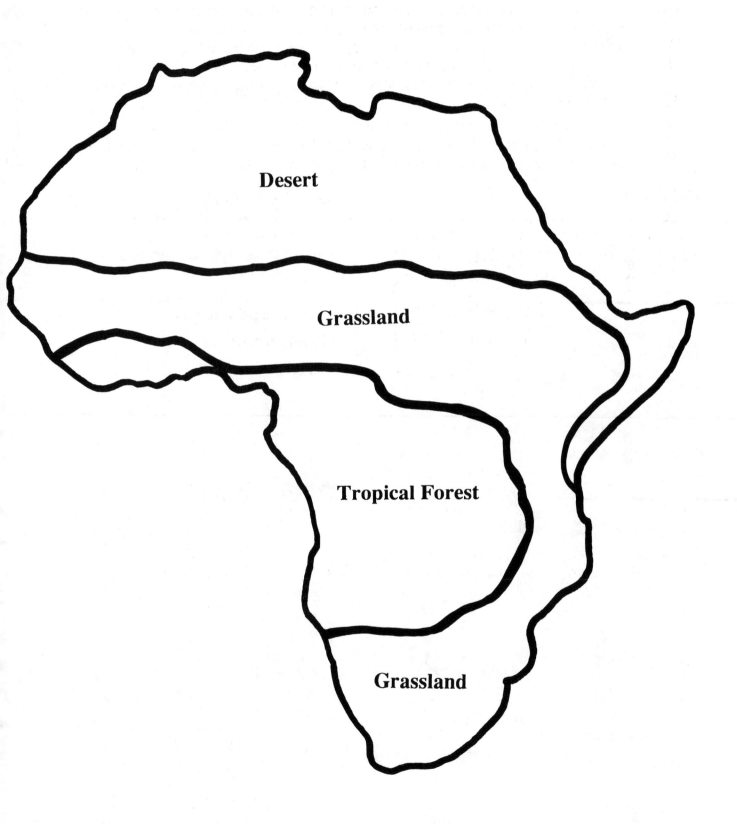

Desert

Grassland

Tropical Forest

Grassland

ANIMALS

Historical Aid

Africa has thousands of kinds of mammals, reptiles, amphibians, fishes, birds and insects. The most populous animal habitats on the continent are the deserts, grasslands *(savanna),* and tropical forests. Some species can also be found in the swamps, streams and sparse mountainous ranges.

The number and kinds of animals were previously more diverse and widespread. Ancient paintings on rocks show that hippopotamus and giraffes once lived in regions that are now deserts. Gradual changes in climate and growth of cities have destroyed some of the natural environment on which the animals depend. Uncontrolled hunting has also contributed to the decline in Africa's animal population.

PROJECT

Create a mural that reflects the natural habitats in which the animal population lives on the African continent.

MATERIALS

- Large topographical map of Africa, see pages 6-7
- White construction paper or other painting paper
- Tempera paint and brushes
- Crayons
- Scissors
- Glue

DIRECTIONS

1. Make animal reference books available on a resource table.

2. Reproduce several copies of the animal habitat page, following. Review the contents together.

3. Paint or color animals based on the pictures in the reference books. Cut them out and glue them in their natural habitat on the large map. There can be duplicates!

ANIMALS OF AFRICA

GRASSLANDS

Much of inland Africa is dry savanna, with short grasses and thorn-trees. The vast stretches of open country are home to many of the largest and swiftest animals.

lion
elephant
gazelle
zebra
cheetah
giraffe
rhinoceros
impala
gnu
wildebeest
aardvark
eland
okapi
leopard
hyena
jackal
serval
buffalo
kudu
ostrich
vulture

TROPICAL FORESTS

Animals of the tropical rain forests have an environment that is always hot and wet. Swamps, rivers and small mountain ranges are found within the rain forest habitat.

monkey	hippopotamus
leopard	baboon
chimpanzee	ibis
toucan	flamingo
mountain gorilla	pelican
python	storks
crocodile	

DESERTS

A great deal of North Africa is dry and barren desert with scrub and grass suitable for pasture only part of the time. Most of the animals can live without water for several days.

dromedary	jerboa
Tennec fox	jackal
porcupine	hyena
vulture	sheep
	cattle
	goat
	ostrich

AFRICAN VILLAGE

Historical Aid

Most large cities in Africa have homes and apartments that resemble those in other cities, but a large part of the African population still lives in traditional dwellings. The types of houses in which people live depend upon the region and the climate.

Along the coast in West Africa people live in houses built on stilts. In Chad the homes have walls made with grass and mud, topped with thatched roofs. The Dogon tribes from Mali build their houses of woven straw and mud, perching them on rugged mountain sides. Nomadic tribes like the Masai construct their houses of sticks, mud and cow dung. Whenever they need to move, they simply take the houses apart to move with them.

PROJECT

Make a replica of an African thatched roof village.

DIRECTIONS

1. Cut the oatmeal box in half. Cut out a door. Paint earthtone color.

2. Make a cone for roof and glue on the top of the oatmeal box.

3. Use green and brown paint to decorate the roof, or cover with straw or small sticks.

4. Arrange huts on a covered table top. Decorate the village with sticks for a wood pile, rocks for a cooking fire, and put dirt and grass throughout the village.

5. Make village people out of clay. Paint the clay figures to show different types of African dress.

6. Use dirt and grass to make a field for growing crops, and clay to make a herd of cattle.

7. Make trees for the village with green and brown construction paper.

MATERIALS

- Oatmeal boxes
- Brown and green construction paper
- Earthtone, brown and green tempera paint
- Glue
- Scissors
- Clay
- Small sticks, dirt, rocks and grass

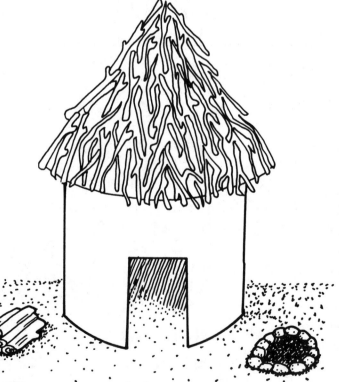

© Edupress

GANVIE VILLAGE

Historical Aid

In the middle of Lake Nohoui in the country of Benin is the town of Ganvie. The town is a cluster of houses built on stilts. This type of house is very practical in an area covered by lagoons and marshlands, as the stilts raise the level of the houses a few feet above the surface of the water.

Palm wood sticks tied together in a crisscross pattern form the walls, and the roofs are thatched with layers of straw. The primary means of transportation in this area is by dugout canoes, which are used for fishing as well as for traveling from house to house.

PROJECT

Create a Ganvie Village.

DIRECTIONS

Paint large piece of butcher paper blue. Cut into shape of lake.

Cut top off of milk carton. Cut four slits in bottom of carton, large enough to accommodate craft sticks. Push sticks into the slits to form stilts, carefully adjusting lengths to keep house balanced.

Cut piece of brown construction paper to cover outside of milk carton. Use black marker to make crisscross designs on paper and glue paper to carton.

Cut cardboard to form flat roof and lay on top of milk carton. Glue dried grass or straw on roof for thatched appearance.

Place completed houses on butcher paper lake. Decorate scene as desired with canoes or other village details.

MATERIALS

- Butcher paper
- Blue tempera paint
- Milk carton
- Craft sticks
- Black marker
- Glue
- Cardboard
- Dried grass or straw
- Brown construction paper

KENTE CLOTH

Historical Aid

The Ashanti tribe of Ghana in West Africa originally made kente cloth for their kings. Kente cloth is a brilliantly colored fabric which is made by weaving intricate patterns in strips, and then sewing the strips together. It can be made out of silk, cotton or rayon.

Today kente cloth is the national dress of Ghana. It is used to make robes, called *kento*, that drape around the body, or turban-like headdresses called *gele*. Women wear *lapas* which are skirts that tie around the waist. Kente cloth is woven by men on small looms, often under the shade of a big tree. Red, green, yellow, white, blue, and black are colors found in kente cloth.

PROJECT

Create a bulletin board made up of kente cloth design squares.

MATERIALS

- Scissors
- Coloring page, following
- Colored markers

DIRECTIONS

1. Reproduce kente cloth designs on page 13.
2. Color with markers and cut out.
3. Put the finished designs together on a bulletin board to look like a finished length of kente cloth.

KENTE CLOTH

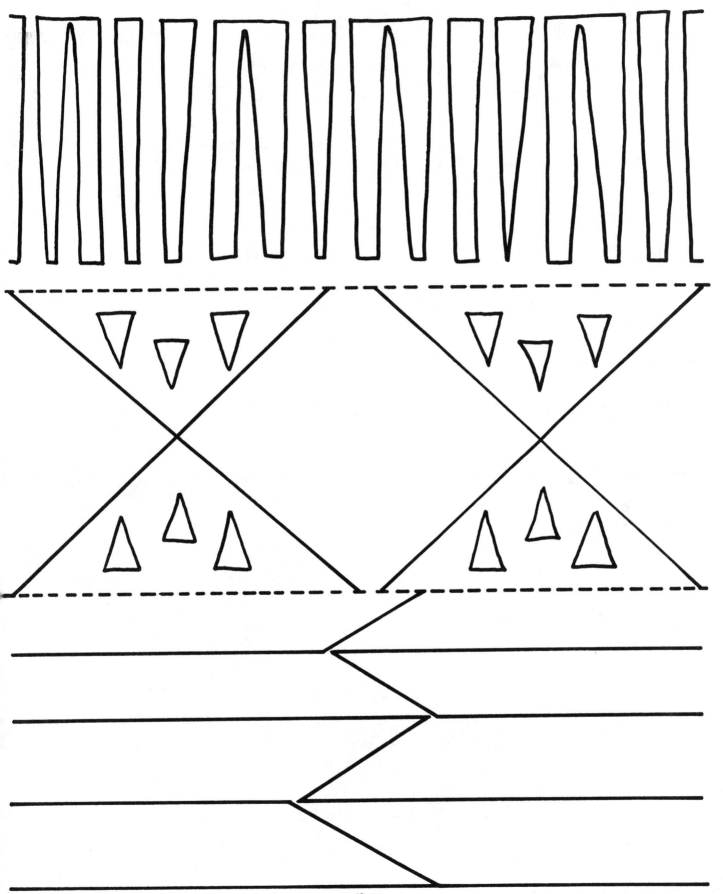

ADINKRA CLOTH

Historical Aid

The Ashanti people of Ghana paint and stamp patterns on woven fabrics used for garments. In earlier times, the symbolic designs were stamped on dark cloth and worn only at funerals to express grief. Now people are stamping adinkra patterns on lighter fabrics and wearing them for other occasions.

The stamps used in making adinkra cloth are carved from pieces of calabash gourd, then dipped in thick ink and stamped on woven cloth. Each design has a special meaning. When a person wears adinkra cloth, he or she is sending a message.

PROJECT

Prepare fabric or butcher paper with adinkra designs for use in making the *dashiki* or *gele* on page 16.

DIRECTIONS

1. Trace each stencil on a sponge and cut out either with scissors or an art knife.

2. Lay the butcher paper or the fabric out on newspaper. Tape the ends down.

3. Put different colors of paint in each pie pan. Dip the sponges in the paint and print on the cloth.

MATERIALS

- Sponges, preferably flat ones that puff up in water
- Butcher paper, or fabric, cut in 12 x 36-inch (37 cm x 100 cm) pieces
- Tempera paint
- Scissors or art knife
- Thin, dark marker for tracing
- Pie tins for paint
- Newspaper

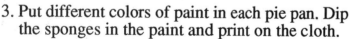

ADINKRA CLOTH

DASHIKI & GELE

Historical Aid

One type of shirt worn by African men for religious ceremonies and festivals is called a *dashiki*. This is a loosely fitting shirt with an open neck and flowing sleeves. It is made of brightly colored woven fabric with adinkra designs printed on it. Women in some West African countries wear long *dashiki*-type dresses for special occasions.

African women often wear a wrapped headdress called a *gele*. The *gele* is useful in protecting their heads from the intense heat, and in cushioning them against the heavy loads they often carry on their heads.

PROJECT

Design and create a *dashiki* or a *gele*.

MATERIALS

• Adinkra cloth or butcher paper prepared on page 14

DIRECTIONS-DASHIKI

1. Fold fabric or butcher paper in half lengthwise.
2. Cut neck opening in the folding edge large enough for a head to fit through.

DIRECTIONS-GELE

1. Place fabric so that it is centered at back of head. The two ends should be even when you bring them to the front.
2. Bring the two ends forward and overlap in front. Bring ends to back and tie a knot at base of head.
3. Bring the loose ends back to the front, cross them and tuck into the front or sides of the *gele*.

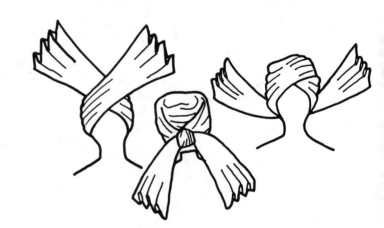

BATIK & TIE-DYING

Historical Aid

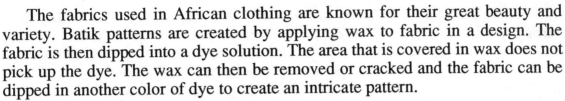

The fabrics used in African clothing are known for their great beauty and variety. Batik patterns are created by applying wax to fabric in a design. The fabric is then dipped into a dye solution. The area that is covered in wax does not pick up the dye. The wax can then be removed or cracked and the fabric can be dipped in another color of dye to create an intricate pattern.

In Nigeria the Baule tribe uses a special method of fabric design called *adire*, or tie-dying. Fabric is tied tightly with string and dipped in dye. Those sections that are tied do not receive the dye, creating a pattern. Dyes are created from native plants and trees.

PROJECT

Create a fabric design using batik or tie-dying.

MATERIALS

• White cotton fabric cut in 10-inch (25 cm) squares

DIRECTIONS–BATIK

Additional materials: Crayons, electric frying pan, soup cans, paint brushes, iron, newsprint

1. Put crayons into empty soup cans.

2. Melt crayons by putting cans into electric frying pan. Fill pan ¼ full of water and turn to high heat.

3. When crayons are melted turn the heat to low. Carefully remove the cans. Have the students paint a design on their fabric with paint brushes. If the crayons start to harden return the can to frying pan until crayons are fully melted.

4. When designs are completed have an adult iron the batik. Use newsprint on both sides of the batik to absorb the excess wax.

DIRECTIONS–TIE-DYING

Additional materials: Various colors of dye, bowls, rubber bands, rubber gloves

1. Mix dye in bowls per package instructions.

2. Take a small section of fabric and tightly wrap a rubber band around it in several places.

3. Wearing rubber gloves, dip the fabric in the dye. (The dye will work immediately. The longer it stays in the dye the darker the pattern color will be.)

4. When fabric is dark enough, remove from dye and carefully remove rubber bands. Lay fabric flat to dry.

AFRICAN COOKING
Historical Aid

Traditional tribal custom is to eat only one large meal a day, with light snacks throughout the day. The main meal is a time for socializing with relatives and neighbors, although the men and boys usually eat separately from the women and girls. In many households, the people gather around a large bowl of food set on the ground and scoop up the food with their fingers or with pieces of bread.

Although foods differ from region to region, some are common throughout most of Africa; corn, cassava (a starchy root used as a base for tapioca), yams, and bananas are typical.

PROJECT

Divide into cooperative groups to cook and eat a meal with recipes adapted from authentic African recipes.

MATERIALS

- Ingredients as listed in recipes following
- Cooking utensils and pans
- Stove or cooktop
- Individual serving bowls
- Bread
- Materials for clean-up

DIRECTIONS

1. Divide into three cooperative groups.

2. Reproduce and cut apart the recipe page. Give each group a recipe to prepare for a classroom meal.

3. Divide food into individual portions in serving bowls and give each child a slice of bread.

4. Spread a large sheet on the ground for seating and enjoying the meal. Remember to scoop the food with the bread instead of eating utensils!

RECIPES

JOLLOF RICE

Jollof rice comes from West Africa and is thought to be named after the Jollof region of Senegal. "Jollof" always means the rice is cooked in the dish rather than separately.

INGREDIENTS:
- 1 chicken, cut up
- 2 small cans tomatoes
- 2 cups (500 ml) water
- salt & pepper to taste
- 1 cup (250 ml) uncooked rice
- 1/4 tsp (1 ml) each cinnamon & ground red pepper
- 3 cups (750 ml) coarsely shredded cabbage
- 1 cup (250 ml) sliced green beans
- 2 onions, sliced

DIRECTIONS:
Heat chicken, tomatoes (with liquid), water, salt and pepper to boiling in a large pan. Reduce heat. Cover and simmer 30 minutes. Remove chicken. Stir in rice, cinnamon and red pepper. Add remaining ingredients and return to boil. Reduce heat, cover and simmer until chicken is done, 20 to 30 minutes.

YAMS

Yams are grown in many sections of Africa and are the main food source for many African families. Yams are common in West and Central Africa. They can be boiled or fried. In Nigeria a fried yam snack food is called "small chop".

BOILED YAMS:
Peel yams and place in a pan with water to cover. Add a small amount of salt and bring to a boil. Cook until tender. Drain. Mash with sugar and butter to taste.

FRIED YAMS:
Peel yams and slice. Fry in hot oil. Serve in small paper cups.

BANANA BAKE

Bananas baked with brown sugar, fruit juices and coconut provide a welcome refreshment after a spicy African meal. This recipe is from Ghana, and its African name is "akwadu".

INGREDIENTS:
- 5 medium bananas
- 1 Tbsp (15 ml) butter
- ⅓ cup (80 ml) orange juice
- 1 Tbsp (15 ml) lemon juice
- 3 Tbsp (45 ml) packed brown sugar
- ⅔ cup (160 ml) shredded coconut

DIRECTIONS:
Cut bananas crosswise into halves; cut each lengthwise in half again. Arrange in greased pie plate. Dot with butter and drizzle with juices. Sprinkle with brown sugar and coconut. Bake at 375° F (190° C) until coconut is golden, 8 to 10 minutes.

MAGIC BEADED DOLL

Historical Aid

The Sotho tribe of southern Africa has a custom that all brides must follow. When a young girl marries she carries a magic beaded doll. This doll has a cone-shaped body which is decorated with beads. It has no arms or legs, and is adorned with earrings. The bride must give the doll a name, and later she is to name her first-born child after the doll.

PROJECT

Make a magic beaded doll.

MATERIALS

- Light cardboard
- Black yarn
- Black paint
- 2-inch (5.4 cm) foam ball
- Beads
- Burlap

DIRECTIONS

1. Make a cone by tracing the pattern on the cardboard piece. Cut, fold and glue the ends.

2. Paint the foam ball black. When dry, paint a face on the ball.

3. Use the black yarn as hair and attach beads to the ends of the hair.

4. Using yarn, make circle earrings and attach to the sides of the ball.

5. Decorate the body with beads and use the small piece of burlap as a cape.

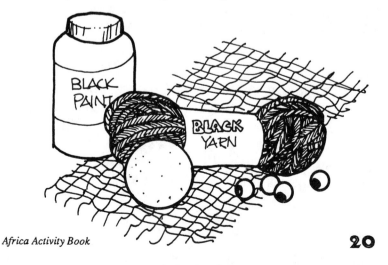

MAGIC BEADED DOLL

MASKS

Historical Aid

In Africa masks have been used throughout the centuries in ceremonial dances. These masks can be very elaborate and intricately decorated. Each tribe has its own unique masks made from a variety of materials. Some are carved from wood. Others utilize natural materials such as hide, grass or shells. Many are painted with symbolic designs and colors. Zambian mask-makers combine bark and mud to create ferocious faces they paint in black, red and white.

Among some peoples there are special masked societies whose members dance wearing masks and costumes. Dancers at Egungun wear masks simulating animal heads.

PROJECT

Select from the masks described on the following page and choose one to make.

As an optional activity students may form cooperative groups and select one type of mask to research and make. They may present their research in an oral presentation to classmates.

MATERIALS

• Gather materials as needed for each mask described on the following page.

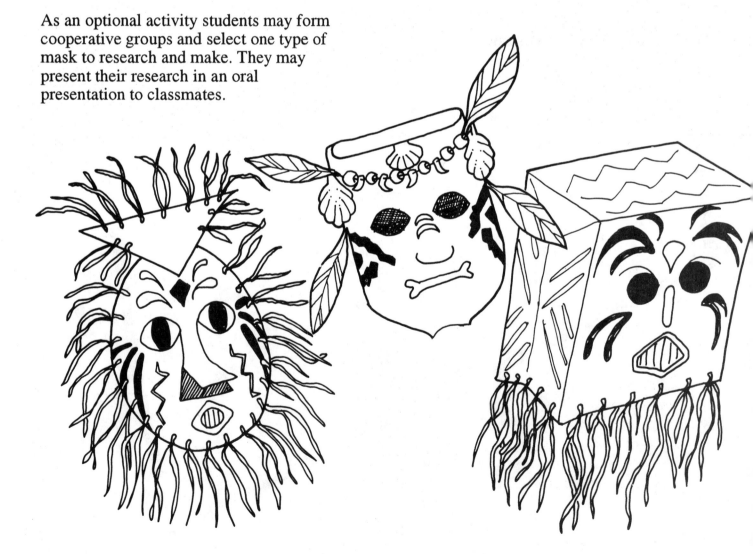

AFRICAN MASKS

BASONGA

The Basonga tribe of the Congo River region make masks with elaborately painted faces to wear in ceremonial dances. They also create special masks for celebrating their harvest festival. These harvest masks are decorated with shells, feathers, beads and bones.

Ceremonial Mask

Cut a ten-inch (27 cm) **tagboard** oval for each mask. Sketch a face or design on the oval Color with **marking pens**. Cut around the nose and bend forward. Cut a geometric **construction paper** shape. **Staple** to the top. Use a **hole punch** to make holes around the edges. Tie with strips of **yarn, raffia or tissue paper.**

Harvest Mask

Cut the back half (including pour spout) off a **plastic jug**. Cut eye holes. Use **tempera paint** in assorted colors to make African symbols or designs. **Glue beads, shells, feathers, foil, glitter or dried bones** to decorate. Cut a slot on each side and tie **yarn** to hold the mask on the head.

DOGON

Spirit Mask

The Dogon tribe of West Africa wears bright masks in a ceremonial dance to scare away the spirits of the dead. These masks are rectangular in shape with a bright ruffle around the neck.

Fit a large brown **paper grocery bag** to the child's head. Draw the eyes with **marking pen**. Use **scissors** to cut the eyeholes. Decorate using **paint** and marking pens. Use a **hole punch** to make holes at two-inch (5 cm) intervals around the bottom of the grocery bag. Tie bright **tissue paper** strips through the holes.

TRIBAL SHIELDS

Historical Aid

Shields were made in a great variety of sizes and shapes. Some were only a few inches long and were carried in dance rituals. Others were used by the African warriors to protect themselves from the spears of their enemies or the claws and teeth of wild animals.

Shields were made from various materials that were readily available. The shapes varied from tribe to tribe. The Zulu tribe made long painted shields and covered them with goat hide. In Kenya the Masai made their shields shorter and covered them with cow hide. The shield was then painted with designs.

PROJECT

Design and create a tribal shield.

MATERIALS

- Thick tagboard
- Markers and tempera paint
- Tape
- Scissors
- Tag board strips
- Glitter, feathers and sequins

DIRECTIONS

1. Cut the tagboard into the shape of the shield you choose to make.

2. Decorate in African patterns or animal fur designs.

3. Tape tagboard strips to the back of the shield as a handle.

SPEAR

Historical Aid

The spear of a Masai warrior is his most precious possession. The spear has a long wooden handle, with a sharp steel tip and a steel piece at the base of the handle. The metal is polished daily with animal fat to prevent rusting. A Masai warrior keeps his spear with him at all times, either in his hand or nearby, thrust into the ground with the point up. At night it is stored inside the living quarters.

These spears are not only used for fighting, but are sometimes decorated to symbolize peace. Black ostrich feathers are attached to the tip of the spear with a string of beads.

PROJECT

Make a replica of a Masai spear decorated as a peace symbol.

DIRECTIONS

1. Cut a long spear head out of cardboard.

2. Cover with aluminum foil.

3. Attach this with masking tape to the cardboard tube.

4. Paint the cardboard section of the spear. Decorate with African designs.

5. Cut a feather from construction paper and fringe. Glue to the tip of the spear.

MATERIALS

• Aluminum foil

• Long cardboard wrapping paper tube

• Masking tape

• Bright-colored paint

• Black construction paper

• Scissors

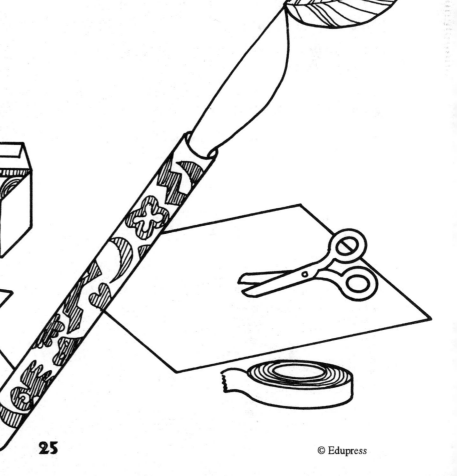

MASAI LION MANES

Historical Aid

Killing a lion wins a Masai warrior the animal's mane to be made into a ceremonial headdress. The headdresses are stylized to signify bravery in killing lions or enemy warriors.

In a ceremony known as *Eunoto*, held once every seven years, Masai warriors are chosen to become tribal elders. For the ceremony warriors don their lion-mane headdresses for the last time and smear white chalk from a sacred cliff on their faces and bodies.

PROJECT

Create a lion-mane headdress.

MATERIALS

- Natural-colored raffia or yellow yarn
- Markers or tempera paint
- Construction paper cut in 2-inch (5 cm) strips
- Scissors
- Glue

DIRECTIONS

1. Decorate a paper strip in African patterns using markers or paint.

2. Staple raffia or yarn to the strip to resemble a lion's mane.

3. Wrap the mane around the head and staple together at the back of the head.

4. Wear the mane with Masai shield and paint face with white chalk for a Masai tribal ceremony.

CEREMONIAL DRESS

Historical Aid

Ceremonial dancing is an important part of the tribal life for the Zulu and Dogon tribesmen in east and west Africa. Masks, shields and spears are part of the ceremony.

Garments worn in the dances vary from tribe to tribe. The Masai ceremonial dress is a large piece of decorated cloth wrapped around the dancers' bodies. Dancers from the Zulu tribe wear skirts made from raffia, fiber from the leaves of a palm tree native to the island of Madagascar.

PROJECT

Make a Zulu ceremonial dance skirt.

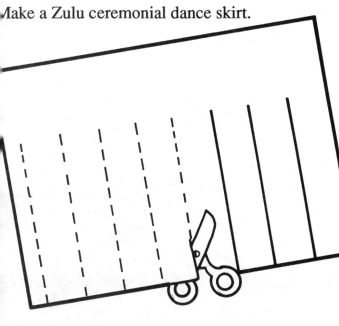

MATERIALS

- Brown butcher paper
- Heavy yarn or rope
- Scissors
- Masking tape

DIRECTIONS

1. Cut the yarn or rope into lengths to fit around each student's waist plus 12 inches (30 cm).

2. Cut a length of butcher paper long enough to fit around the waist and wide enough to reach just above the knees.

3. Fringe the butcher paper leaving a two-inch (5 cm) strip uncut at the top.

4. Fold the uncut portion in half and wrap it around the rope. Approximately six inches of rope or yarn should extend beyond each end of the butcher paper.

5. Tape the folded edge to the back of the skirt.

6. To wear the skirt, tie the rope together in the back.

AFRICAN SHAKERS

Historical Aid

Music is a valued part of African daily life. Music is made by the singing voice and by musical instruments made from natural materials. Flutes, trumpets and other wind instruments are made from wood, reeds or metal. Stringed instruments are often made using gourds for the sound-boxes. Even a hunting bow can become a kind of violin. Shakers (*ishakas*) can be made of long tubes of straw or sugar cane filled with seeds, beans, pebbles or sand. Each has a different sound. The *shekere* is an instrument made from a dried calabash gourd wrapped in loose mesh with beads attached to the mesh.

PROJECT

Design and make African shakers.

DIRECTIONS

SHEKERE

1. Put beans in balloon. Blow balloon up and tie it.

2. Tape a wooden dowel or cardboard roll to the end of the balloon.

3. Mix 3 parts liquid starch with 1 part white glue. Dip small pieces of newsprint in the starch mixture and place on the balloon. Cover the entire balloon and the top part of the wooden dowel.

4. Allow the starch mixture to dry for about 24 hours. Paint the shakers with African design.

ISHAKAS

1. Tape one end of a wrapping paper tube closed and put a handful of beans inside.

2. Tape the other side of the tube closed.

3. Paint in African colors and designs.

MATERIALS

- Medium-sized balloons
- Wooden dowels cut in 6-inch (16 cm) pieces or thick cardboard rolled into a 6-inch (16 cm) long roll and taped
- Brown, black, yellow, purple and green paint
- Wrapping paper tubes
- Small pieces of newsprint
- Tape
- White glue
- Starch
- Beans

TRIBAL DRUMS

Historical Aid

The drum is a common musical instrument all over Africa. Many years ago important messages were sent between tribes or distant villages by drum. Now Africans use more modern ways of communicating, but drums are still a very important part of tribal dances and ceremonies.

African drums can be made from many different types of materials. These include tree trunks, elephant tusks, clay and tortoise shell. The drums usually have an animal hide stretched over the top, although the slit drum is a carved wooden piece with slits at the top. When hit with a wooden stick the slit drum makes a deep resonant sound.

PROJECT

Design and make an African drum.

DIRECTIONS

Cut butcher paper to cover sides of container(s).

Paint butcher paper desired color or design.

Tape lid to container. Cover open top with a circle of construction paper which is two inches (5 cm) larger in circumference than opening. Affix with rubber band.

Decorate drum with beads and raffia.

To make long drums, glue two oatmeal cartons together and cover. You can attach shoulder straps by making holes in container(s) before covering and threading yarn through the openings.

MATERIALS

- Butcher paper
- Tempera paint
- Tape
- Scissors
- Rubber bands
- Beads, raffia, yarn
- Oatmeal box or ice cream carton with lid
- Colored pens. glitter, feathers and sequins

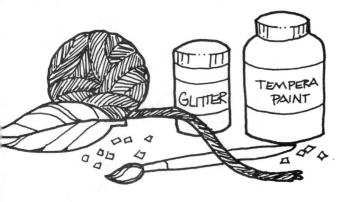

XYLOPHONE

Historical Aid

 Music and dance combine in symbolic rituals and cultural occasions throughout Africa. In addition to drums, percussion instruments such as bells, the xylophone and the "thumb piano" *(likembe)* are also used to make sounds and rhythms. The thumb piano seems to come from Lower Zaire but has spread south to Angola, Zambia and South Africa. A portable xylophone, originating in the Congo, was often taken by a chief when traveling.

Zambian dancers form two lines, men in one row, women in another. The addition of bells and rattles to their wrists and ankles adds to the melodic sounds created by drums, flutes, xylophones, and thumb pianos.

PROJECT

Construct a portable xylophone and participate in a Zambian line dance.

DIRECTIONS

1. Clean the cans and remove both ends.

2. Use marking pens to draw African designs around the edge of the box lid or base.

3. Punch a hole at opposite ends of the box sides, about ½ inch (1.27 cm) from the top edge.

4. Cut a length of yarn long enough to go around the neck and reach to the waist. Thread a yarn end through opposite holes and tie a knot to hold them in place.

5. Each child should select a combination of three or more cans and blocks. The number and size will depend on the size of the box.

6. Arrange the cans and blocks in the box. The cans should be on their sides. Glue them in place in the box. When dry, wear the xylophone around the neck and strike the cans and blocks with a dowel or drumming stick to create different tones and sounds.

MATERIALS

- Wood dowel or drumming stick
- Large lightweight gift box (lid or base)
- Empty cans and blocks of wood in varying sizes
- Yarn
- Scissors
- Hole punch
- Marking pens
- Tacky glue

MANKALA

Historical Aid

Mankala is a game which is played in East Africa. The same game is played in Western and South Africa but it is called *Oware, Ayi* or *Ware. Mankala* is a game in which two players move pieces from one cup to another until there are no more left to move. The winner is the player with the most pieces in his cup.

Mankala boards are often carved out of wood and are ornately decorated. However, in some parts of Africa the twelve holes of the game are dug in the sand and pebbles are used as playing pieces.

PROJECT

Create a *Mankala* game board to play with a friend.

DIRECTIONS

Decorate the top of the egg carton with markers or paint.

Tape paper cups to the ends of the open egg carton.

Place four playing pieces in each of the twelve cups of the egg carton.

GAME RULES

Two players sit so that six cups are in front of each player. Player #1 picks up four beans from any of the cups. Beginning with the cup to the left of the cup he empties, the player drops one bean in each cup, going counterclockwise, until all the beans in his hand are gone. The second player does the same thing. If a player drops his last bean in a cup with at least two or more beans in it, he wins all the beans in that cup. He puts his winnings in his cup at the end of the board.

The game continues until there are no more beans left in any of the twelve cups. Each player counts the beans in his end cup. The player with the most beans wins.

MATERIALS

• Egg carton

• Markers and tempera paint

• Tape

• Scissors

• 48 dried beans, buttons or stones

• Two paper cups

JEWELRY
Historical Aid

Jewelry is a very important part of the African culture. Many Africans consider ornate jewelry a part of their everyday costume. African jewelry may signify whether the wearer is available for marriage, whether he is wealthy, what tribe the wearer comes from, and his age. It may even signify brave deeds in battle or heroic deeds in daily life.

Jewelry can be made of almost any material. Copper, silver, brass, wooden beads, glass beads, amber, bones, feathers, shells and gold are commonly used. Jewelry may even be made of woven palm leaves or elephant tail hair.

PROJECT

Use household items to make replicas of African jewelry.

MATERIALS

• Jewelry instruction page, following
• Materials listed for individual projects

DIRECTIONS

1. Reproduce and cut apart jewelry project page. Post each project in a different area in an "African Jewelry Center".

2. Demonstrate each project to the children and leave it in the center as a reference sample.

3. Children may make one or all of the projects. Provide time for children to share their projects with classmates.

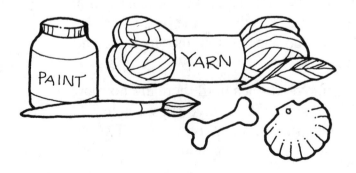

BEAD NECKLACE

MATERIALS
- One cup (250 ml) each flour and salt
- Water
- Paint • Yarn

DIRECTIONS:
1. Mix flour and salt with enough water to form clay.
2. Shape clay into beads, using a toothpick to make a hole. Bake at 200° F (92° C) until hard. Paint.
3. String beads on yarn.

NATURE NECKLACE

MATERIALS
- Shells, beads, bones
- Fishing line or dental floss

DIRECTIONS:
1. Cut floss or fishing line to the desired length.
2. Tie or string natural objects at intervals on the floss.

ELEPHANT HAIR NECKLACE

MATERIALS
- Pliers
- Black nylon cord or black yarn
- Thin wire or gold-colored jewelry fasteners

DIRECTIONS:
1. Use black cord or yarn to make several wrist-size loops.
2. Wrap pieces of wire or a fastener around the loops at one-inch (2.54 cm) intervals, using pliers to tighten.

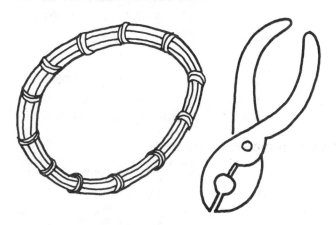

NOK SCULPTURE

Historical Aid

The oldest known African sculptures are terra cotta (clay) figures created by the Nok civilization in central Nigeria. The Nok were a West African civilization that flourished from about 500 B.C. until 200 A.D. Today Nok is the name of a village in Nigeria, about 100 miles (160 km) northeast of Baro.

The sculptures of animal and human figures vary in size from 1 inch (2.5 cm) high to life size. All the human heads have pierced ears and the eyes are hollowed out.

PROJECT

Sculpt a clay figure having the characteristics of those created during the Nok civilization.

DIRECTIONS

1. Sculpt an animal or human figure.
2. If a human figure is sculpted be sure the eyes are hollowed out. Use a toothpick to pierce the ears. Add sequin or bead earrings.
3. Paint a terra cotta (rust) shade. Fire in the kiln or allow to harden.

OPTIONAL ACTIVITY:

1. Make life-size "sculptures" by working in pairs to trace each other's outline on a large sheet of butcher paper. Cut around the outline.
2. Blend tempera paint to create a terra cotta (rust) shade. Paint the cut paper shape and add facial features, including sunken eyes and earrings.

MATERIALS

- Clay—self-hardening or other available
- Toothpicks
- Sequins or other small beads

OPTIONAL ACTIVITY MATERIALS:

- Butcher paper
- Crayons
- Red, black and white tempera paint
- Scissors, paint brush

GALIMOTOS

Historical Aid

African children are very resourceful when it comes to making toys and games. Their toys are made from items they can find around their village or from natural materials within their environment.

One toy that southern African children have learned to make is called a "Galimoto". This is a push toy built from scraps of wood and metal to resemble a car, motorcycle, truck or any other vehicle with a motor.

PROJECT

Design and build a "Galimoto".

DIRECTIONS

Use wood and metal materials to create a vehicle.

Attach a long wire or stick to use to push the toy.

Have a "Galimoto" parade around the room.

MATERIALS

- Scraps of wire, wooden dowels, pipe cleaners, sticks, cardboard pieces, scrap metal, tongue depressors or popsicle sticks, metal coat hangers
- Glue
- Tape
- Scissors, wire cutters

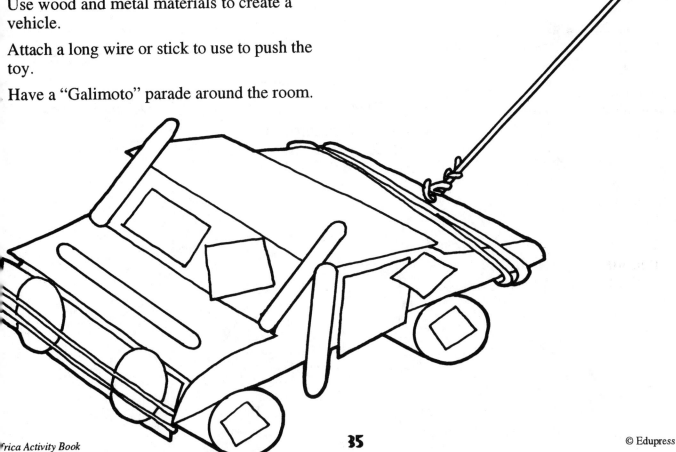

IVORY

Historical Aid

The tusks of some animals are made of a hard, creamy-white substance called *ivory*. Some ivory comes from the tusks, horns and teeth of the hippopotamus but the most valued comes from the tusks of African elephants. In order to obtain the ivory the elephant must be killed because one third of the tusk is embedded in the skull. The African elephant was hunted almost into extinction.

An average elephant tusk is six feet (two meters) in length and weighs 50 pounds (23 kg). Early Africans used the ivory to carve small objects such as spoons, small dishes, horns and bracelets. The Obo tribe of Benin still carves intricate designs on ivory to surround the shrines built for their ancestors.

PROJECT

"Carve" ivory and create a necklace.

MATERIALS

- Foam meat or produce trays from the market
- Yarn
- Scissors
- Nail
- Toothpick

DIRECTIONS

1. Use the toothpick to outline several shapes in the foam tray.

2. Cut out around the outline. Use the toothpick again to "carve" lines and designs in the cut-out.

3. Carefully poke the nail through the foam pieces to create a hole in each.

4. Thread a length of yarn through the styrofoam pieces, spacing them at different intervals. Tie around the neck to wear.

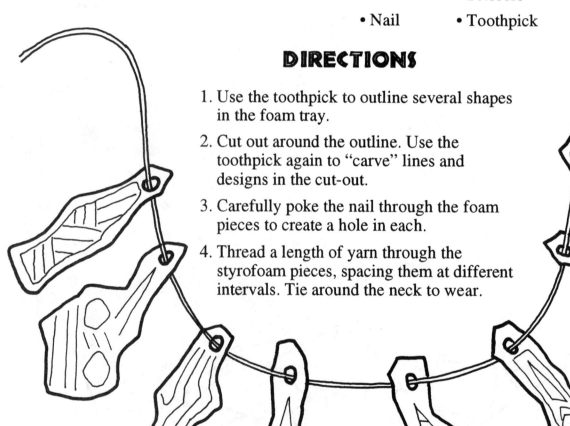

NOMADIC TRIBES

Historical Aid

The Tuareg people are a nomadic tribe who for centuries have traveled the Sahara desert with their herds of camels, goats, sheep and cattle. They move about following the seasonal rainfall, living in tents made of goatskin or mats woven from palm leaves.

In the past the Tuareg developed trade routes back and forth across the Sahara. Caravans carried gold, ivory, kola nuts and parrots to trade for cloth, rugs and metals. Being an artistic people, they have left samples of their artwork in beautiful jewelry and in carvings made on rocks across the desert.

PROJECT

Make a sandpaper drawing of a Tuareg caravan.

DIRECTIONS

Have students draw picture of camels and riders in the desert. Make sure they press hard with crayons.

Cover picture with newsprint.

Iron newsprint with hot iron to melt crayon. Carefully peel back newsprint.

MATERIALS

- Sandpaper
- Crayons
- Hot iron
- Newsprint

GRISGRIS

Historical Aid

The Tuareg people of the Sahara desert traveled great distances across the desert to bring back silver. Their main trade route was across the desert to Tripoli, the Gateway of Africa.

The silver was molded onto camel hide to make amulets which the Taureg believed would protect them from illness and misfortune. These good luck charms were called *grisgris*.

PROJECT

Design and make a *grisgris*.

DIRECTIONS

1. Glue string in patterns on the cardboard.
2. When string dries, cover cardboard with aluminum foil. Use fingers to push foil tightly around string patterns.
3. Color with permanent markers. String with plastic cord or yarn and wear around neck.

MATERIALS

- 4 x 4-inch (10 x 10 cm) square cardboard
- Aluminum foil
- String
- Glue
- Permanent markers
- Plastic cord or yarn

ASHANTI HEADDRESS

Historical Aid

The southwest part of what is now the country of Ghana is home to the Ashanti (Asante). The region is so rich in gold that it came to be known as the *Gold Coast*. The Ashanti used gold dust for money. The visible use of gold during festivals gave a sense of wealth and dignity throughout the various Ashanti groups that make up the kingdom. Many important objects such as sword handles, ornaments, rings and headdresses were also made of gold. According to legend the Ashanti empire was founded when a Golden Stool fell from heaven into the lap of the first king, Osei Tutu. It is still believed that the Golden Stool houses the spirit of the Ashanti people.

PROJECT

Make a "gold-plated" ceremonial headdress as worn by Ashanti chiefs.

MATERIALS

- Cardboard box
- Gold spray paint
- Small macaroni
- Scissors
- Wire cutters
- Glue
- Wire

DIRECTIONS

1. Cut the cardboard box to make a 3 x 5-inch (7.62 cm x 12.7 cm) rectangle.

2. Glue macaroni to the cardboard to create a pattern or design.

3. Cut two 8-inch (20.32 cm) lengths of wire. Poke the wire through the cardboard as shown in the illustration. Bend the ends to hold the wire in place.

4. Spray paint the entire headdress gold (or bright yellow).

5. To dress like an Ashanti chief, slide the headdress on so the wire holds it in place on the side of the head. Tie a sheet or large piece of cloth over one shoulder.

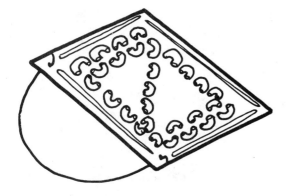

 # SWAHILI
Historical Aid

There are four completely different language types spoken in Africa: Afroasiatic, Khoisan, Nilo-Saharan and Niger Kordofanian. Within each type the there are over 1,000 separate languages, related by vocabulary and grammatical systems. A Niger-Kordofanian language, Kiswahili, is the "mother-tongue" of people along the coast of Kenya and Tanzania and is also spoken by traders over most of East Africa. Kiswahili, more commonly called *Swahili*, has a rich vocabulary containing many words derived from Arabic as well as some from Portuguese and English. English now borrows words from Swahili. Safari is a Swahili word meaning journey and comes from the Arabic word *safara*, travel.

PROJECT

Learn some Swahili words by making a cooperative picture-dictionary mural illustrating Swahili words and learning a Swahili counting song.

DIRECTIONS

1. Copy the Swahili words, including number translations, onto the chalkboard.

2. Each child selects a word to illustrate on the construction paper. Write the Swahili and English translation underneath.

3. Glue the illustration side by side to create a wall mural.

MATERIALS

• Half-sheet white construction paper

• Large sheet butcher paper, any color

• Crayons   • Glue

Swahili	Pronunciation	Meaning
safara	sa-FAR-a	travel
axatse	ox-AHT-see	shaker
baba	BAH-bah	father
mama	MAH-mah	mother
dada	DAH-dah	sister
ndugu	na-DU-gu	brother
chakula	cha-KOO-la	food
fagio	fah-GEE-o	broom
gudulia	goo-DOO-lee-ah	clay jar
jambo	JAM-bo	hello
karibu	ca-REE-bu	welcome
mbira	m-BEER-a	thumb pia
ngoma	na-GO-mah	drum / da
rafiki	rah-FEE-kee	friend
tembo	TEM-bo	elephant
watoto	wah-TOE-toe	children
simba	SIM-bah	lion
shule	SHU-lay	school
kwaheri	kwa-HER-i	goodby
kucheza	koo-CHEZ-a	dance

SWAHILI COUNTING SONG

Na-ma mo-ja mbi-li ta-tu, n-ne, ta-no he-sa bu-ni te-na

Na-ma mo-ja mbi-li ta-tu, n-ne, ta-no he-sa bu-ni te-na

ONE	TWO	THREE	FOUR	FIVE
1	2	3	4	5
moja MO-jah	mbili m-BEE-lee	tatu TA-too	nne N-nay	tano TAH-no

NUMBER	LET'S	COUNT	AGAIN
NAMA	HESA	BUNI	TENA
NA-ma	HAY-sa	BOO-ne	TEN-a

STORYTELLING

Historical Aid

Africa has a great oral tradition among its ethnic groups. The storyteller was a respected person whose words could weave a binding spell while his stories cultivated values and culture to a younger generation. The storyteller would sit for hours at a campfire retelling stories to the people of the village.

Many African stories have animals as main characters. Others, told by tribal elders to their children, tell about their gods and how they wanted people to live. Folk tales and legends are also recounted and passed along from one generation to the next. Many of these can be found published in current children's books. Check the literature list, page 3, for some titles.

PROJECT

Perform an African story in a play form using puppets.

DIRECTIONS

1. Divide class into six groups. Each child in a group will make the same puppet. Trace and cut out puppet patterns on black tagboard.

2. Decorate puppets with craypas, sequins, feather, glitter and beads.

3. Glue wooden dowels to back of puppets.

4. Reproduce and distribute copies of play. The play can be performed as a choral reading or in cooperative groups.

MATERIALS

- Black tagboard
- Craypas (oil pastel crayons)
- Wooden dowels or long pieces of cardboard
- Glue
- Sequins, feathers, glitters and beads
- Patterns for puppets
- Copies of play (pages 46-47)

RABBIT AND THE LONG ONE

NARRATOR - Rabbit came home from work. She was happy to be home. But what was this? Rabbit could not get in her house! Something was in Rabbit's house!

RABBIT - Who is there? Who is in my house?

LONG ONE - I am the Long One, and all are afraid of me because I am great. This is my house now! Go away!

NARRATOR - This made Rabbit afraid. She went to get help. Rabbit found Dog.

RABBIT - Something is in my house. Come and help me.

NARRATOR - So Dog went to Rabbit's house.

DOG - Who is in Rabbit's house?

LONG ONE - I am the Long One, and all are afraid of me because I am great. This is my house now! Go away!

NARRATOR - Dog was afraid, but he said:

DOG - I know what we can do! We can make a fire. That will get rid of the Long One!

RABBIT - That will get rid of my house too! No, no. We can't do that!

NARRATOR - So Rabbit and Dog went to get help. Rabbit and Dog found Elephant.

RABBIT - Something is in my house. Come and help me.

NARRATOR - So Elephant went to Rabbit's house.

ELEPHANT - Who is in Rabbit's house?

LONG ONE - I am the Long One, and all are afraid of me because I am great. This is my house now. Go away!

NARRATOR - Elephant was afraid, but she said:

ELEPHANT - I am big. I will walk on your house Rabbit. That will get rid of the Long One!

RABBIT - That will get rid of my house, too! No, no. You can't do that!

NARRATOR - By now, Rabbit did not know what to do. Dog could not help her. Elephant could not help her. They were all afraid. Who could help her? Just then Frog came by.

FROG - I can help you.

RABBIT - You, Frog? How can you help? You are too little.

FROG - You will see!

NARRATOR - Frog went up to Rabbit's house.

FROG - Who is in Rabbit's house.

LONG ONE - I am the Long One, and all are afraid of me because I am great. This is my house now! Go away!

FROG - I will not go away! I am the Great One. I can do what I want. I can get in that house. And I can get you! Come out! You will not like what I can do.

NARRATOR - Little by little something came out of Rabbit's house. What was it? It was a long, long caterpillar. He looked around.

CATERPILLAR - Where is the Great One? I am just a little thing. I don't want the Great One to get me. I'll go away.

RABBIT - A caterpillar! We were afraid of a caterpillar! Frog, how come you were not afraid?

FROG - Your house is not big, so how could something great and big be in it?

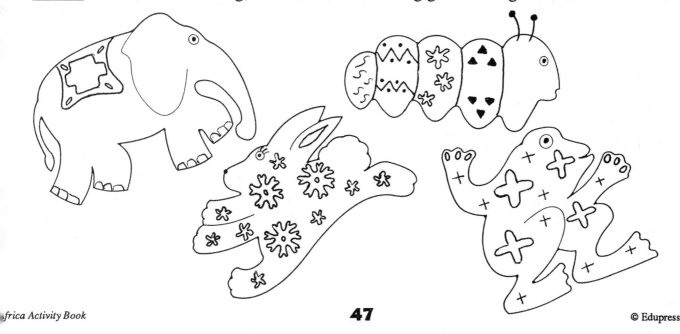

TOE PUPPETS

Historical Aid

African toe puppets were a clever invention from the tribes of West Africa and Mozambique. They were used to pantomime a story, leaving the storyteller's hands free for playing instruments or clapping rhythms.

The original toe puppets were made from bamboo reeds with animal fur for hair. Vines or plant fibers were used to tie the puppets to the puppeteer's big toe. The sizes of the puppets represented their sex. The taller puppets represented the males while the shorter puppets represented the females.

PROJECT

Design and make African toe puppets.

MATERIALS

- Paper towel or toilet paper tubes cut in 4-inch (11 cm) pieces
- Black yarn and string
- Glue
- Scissors
- Scrap fabric
- Colored pens, glitter, feathers and sequins
- Cardboard scraps
- Brads

DIRECTIONS

1. Use markers to draw a face on the tube.

2. Use fabric scraps or markers to make traditional African clothes on the puppet.

3. Cut yarn pieces to desired hair length and glue across the top of the tube.

4. Cut arms out of scrap cardboard and attach to the tube with brads.

5. At ends of the arms make holes. Tie pieces of yarn through the holes. The other end of the yarn will tie on the puppeteer's big toes.

6. String pieces of yarn on the bottom of the cardboard tube. Then string large beads to the yarn for legs. (See recipe for clay beads on page 33.)

7. Have puppeteers clap to African music and wiggle their toes to watch their puppets dance.

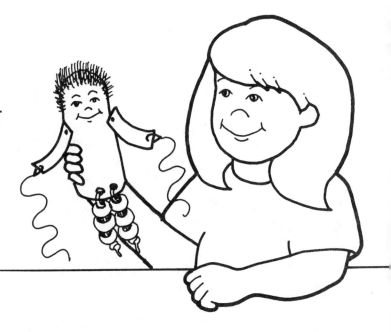